AI MADE EASY

YOUR GUIDE TO UNDERSTANDING ARTIFICIAL INTELLIGENCE

Alex S. Brightman

Table Of Contents

CHAPTER 03. | THE POWER BEHIND AI – DEEP LEARNING AND NEURAL NETWORKS   19

CHAPTER 04. | HOW AI IS USED INBIG BUSINESS   25

CHAPTER 05. | AI IN EVERYDAY LIFE – YOUR PHONE, YOUR HOME, AND BEYOND 32

CHAPTER 06. | AI FOR YOU – MAKING ARTIFICIAL INTELLIGENCE WORK FOR YOU 37

CHAPTER 07. | THE TOOLS OF AI 42

CHAPTER 08. | THE IMPACT OF AI ON WORK 52

CHAPTER 09. | UNLEASHING CREATIVITY WITH AI   58

CHAPTER 10. | ETHICAL CONCERNS AND CHALLENGES   64

CHAPTER 11. | THE ROAD AHEAD   71

CONCLUSION | EMBRACING AI'S POTENTIAL   76

CHAPTER

01

UNDERSTANDING AI

WHAT IS AI, REALLY?

Artificial Intelligence (AI) is often called the technology of the future, but in reality, it's already deeply embedded in our lives. It powers everything from voice assistants like Siri to recommendations on Netflix. But what exactly is AI? Simply put, it refers to machines that can perform tasks that would usually require human intelligence—like understanding language, recognizing images, making decisions, or even creating music.

At its core, AI is all about teaching machines to learn from experience. Instead of giving step-by-step instructions, we let the machines learn by processing data, spotting patterns, and improving over time. Imagine teaching a dog new tricks—not by always saying "sit," but by rewarding it when it sits on its own. Eventually, the dog learns what you expect, and the same principle applies to AI.

AI can be applied in different ways, and understanding these applications is key to seeing just how much it can do. Whether it's a smart fridge that knows when to order more milk or a robot that helps doctors diagnose diseases, AI is transforming industries in ways we never imagined.

THE PIONEERS OF AI: LAYING THE GROUNDWORK

The journey to AI didn't start overnight. In fact, it took decades of hard work and the contributions of some brilliant minds. Among the most important figures in AI's history were **Alan Turing** and **John McCarthy**, two visionaries whose early ideas formed the very foundation of what AI would become.

Alan Turing, an English mathematician and logician, is often called the father of computer science. In the 1930s and 1940s, Turing developed the concept of the "Turing Machine," a theoretical device that could simulate any computer algorithm. Turing also proposed the famous *Turing Test*, which asks whether a machine can imitate human conversation well enough to fool a person into thinking it's human. While Turing's ideas were groundbreaking, he didn't live to see the impact of his work. His theories, however, sparked the development of modern computing and AI.

John McCarthy (1927–2011), an American computer scientist, is another key figure. In 1956, McCarthy organized the famous Dartmouth Conference, which marked the birth of AI as an academic field. It was at this conference that McCarthy, along with others, first proposed the idea that "every aspect of learning or any other feature of intelligence can in principle be so precisely described that a machine can be made to simulate it." McCarthy went on to create the programming language *Lisp*, which became essential for AI research.

These two figures are foundational, but the field of AI didn't really begin to take shape until the 1950s and 1960s, when several other pioneers, including **Marvin Minsky** and **Allen Newell**, began making their mark.

MARVIN MINSKY AND ALLEN NEWELL: THE ARCHITECTS OF AI

Marvin Minsky, often referred to as the father of AI, made profound contributions to the field during his career. Minsky co-founded the MIT Artificial Intelligence Laboratory in 1959, and throughout his life, he was driven by the idea that machines could replicate human thought. His influential book, *The Society of Mind* (1986), argued that human intelligence is not a single ability but a collection of simpler processes, each of which could be simulated by a machine.

Minsky was born in 1927 and spent most of his career at MIT, where his theories shaped much of the early AI research. He famously said, *"The question is not whether intelligent behavior can be made to emerge, but how we can arrange the conditions under which it will emerge."* His optimism about building intelligent machines was ahead of its time, though many of his ideas were not realized until much later due to the limited computing power available at the time.

Allen Newell (1927–1992) was another major figure in the early days of AI. Along with his colleague Herbert Simon, Newell developed the "General Problem Solver" (GPS) in 1956—one of the first AI programs designed to simulate human problem-solving. Their work, which focused on how computers could mimic human reasoning, set the stage for future breakthroughs in artificial intelligence. Newell's legacy also includes his influential research on cognitive psychology, which helped establish the foundations of AI.

Both Minsky and Newell were visionaries, but their optimism about the potential of AI was tempered by the slow pace of technological advancement. In the early years, there was a significant gap between AI's theoretical potential and what computers could actually achieve.

THE SLOW START: AI'S EARLY STRUGGLES

Despite the breakthroughs of Turing, McCarthy, Minsky, and Newell, AI struggled to gain real traction during the 20th century. While the ideas were revolutionary, the technology simply wasn't ready to deliver on them. From the 1950s to the 1970s, AI research was full of ambition but lacked the computational power to achieve its goals. Early systems were slow, limited in scope, and often unable to handle the complexity of real-world tasks.

In the 1970s, AI researchers turned to building "expert systems," which were designed to replicate the decision-making skills of a human expert in specific fields like medicine or engineering. These systems worked by following a set of predefined rules, but they didn't have the ability to learn from new data. Essentially, they were only as smart as the information they were given.

During this time, many experts began to question whether true AI was even possible. The field faced a period of stagnation, often referred to as the "AI winter," where funding dried up and many researchers shifted their focus elsewhere.

THE EXPLOSION OF AI: WHY NOW?

The rapid advancements we see in AI today wouldn't have been possible without key breakthroughs in the 21st century. So, why has AI experienced such explosive growth in recent years? Several factors have come together to make AI far more practical and powerful than ever before.

- 🌐 **Computing Power:** In the early days, AI was constrained by limited hardware. Today, the growth in computing power, particularly through Graphics Processing Units (GPUs), has revolutionized AI. GPUs can process massive amounts of data at incredible speeds, allowing AI systems to learn much more effectively.

- **Big Data:** The digital age has provided a treasure trove of data, much of which is used to train AI systems. From social media to shopping habits, data is everywhere. The availability of this data has made it possible for AI to learn and improve in ways that weren't possible before.

- **Breakthroughs in Deep Learning:** A major development that has propelled AI forward is the advent of deep learning, a technique that mimics the neural networks of the human brain. In 2012, Geoffrey Hinton and his team at the University of Toronto developed a deep learning model that could recognize objects in images far better than previous methods. This breakthrough opened the door for AI to make significant strides in image recognition, natural language processing, and more.

KEY FIGURES DRIVING AI FORWARD

While the early pioneers laid the groundwork, a new generation of researchers and engineers has brought AI into the mainstream. Some of the leading figures today are:

- **Geoffrey Hinton:** Often called the "godfather of deep learning," Geoffrey Hinton's work on neural networks and backpropagation has been instrumental in AI's resurgence. His 2012 victory in the ImageNet competition, where his deep learning model outperformed others in recognizing images, marked a major milestone in the field. Today, Hinton is a professor at the University of Toronto and works with Google Brain, continuing to push the boundaries of AI research.

- **Yann LeCun:** Known for his work on Convolutional Neural Networks (CNNs), Yann LeCun is a professor at New York University and the Chief AI Scientist at Facebook. His innovations in CNNs have made AI systems much better at tasks like image recognition, which is central to many modern AI applications, including facial recognition and self-driving cars.

- **Yoshua Bengio:** Alongside Hinton and LeCun, Yoshua Bengio is often credited as one of the pioneers of deep learning. A professor at the University of Montreal, Bengio's work on unsupervised learning is helping AI systems learn without labeled data, a significant step toward making AI more powerful and flexible.

These researchers, among others, have sparked an AI revolution in the last decade, with applications spanning industries from healthcare to entertainment. Their breakthroughs in deep learning, computing power, and data availability have made AI more practical, scalable, and accessible.

In the next section, we'll dive deeper into the specific applications of AI today and explore how it's transforming businesses and everyday life. But for now, it's important to recognize how far we've come from the early days of AI—thanks to visionaries like Turing, McCarthy, Minsky, Newell, and the new generation of researchers driving this technology forward.

CHAPTER

02

WHAT CAN AI DO? EXPLORING ITS CAPABILITIES

We've spent the first part of our book diving into the history of AI—how it started, the pioneers who made it happen, and how it evolved over time. Now, let's shift gears and talk about what AI can actually do. The technology has made huge leaps in recent years, and its abilities are nothing short of astonishing. In fact, AI is already having a profound effect on both businesses and everyday life.

Whether you're aware of it or not, AI is embedded in so many aspects of our daily routines. From customer service chatbots to personalized entertainment recommendations, AI is quietly working behind the scenes to make our lives easier, faster, and more efficient. Let's take a deeper dive into the many ways AI is already making an impact, and how it's being used to solve real-world problems.

AI IN BIG BUSINESS: REVOLUTIONIZING HOW WE WORK

For years, businesses have been leveraging AI to streamline operations, reduce costs, and improve customer experiences. But the AI revolution is still in its early days, and it's only getting started. Major companies like Amazon, Google, and IBM have been investing in AI for decades, but it's only recently that the impact has become truly transformative.

In the customer service sector, AI has already made huge strides. Virtual assistants and chatbots are now a common feature on many websites and apps, helping businesses automate their customer service operations. Rather than relying on human agents to handle every query, companies are using AI-powered bots to answer questions, solve problems, and even make personalized product recommendations. These bots can process and respond to customer inquiries in real-time, often with little or no input from human staff members. A prime example of this is *IBM Watson*, which has been used in industries ranging from healthcare to finance to improve customer engagement and provide intelligent assistance. The accuracy and efficiency with which these bots handle customer queries has been a game changer, allowing businesses to scale up operations without increasing their workforce.

However, not all AI-powered chatbots are as smooth as a well-brewed cup of coffee. Some of them still have moments that make you wonder if the engineers who built them ever met a human! You know the experience—the chatbot that just doesn't seem to understand simple requests, or worse, gives you a response that's completely off the mark. Ever tried asking a chatbot for help with a billing issue, only to be offered a list of product recommendations instead? It's a bit like asking a librarian for a specific book and getting a completely unrelated one in return, along with a suggestion for a "fascinating" new genre.

But don't be too hard on them! While chatbots have come a long way, they're still learning. AI can be like that one friend who's *very* knowledgeable in some areas but completely clueless in others. Sometimes, they get it right, and other times, they miss the mark by a mile. The problem often lies in the quality of the AI algorithms that individual companies use. Not all AI systems are created equal. Some companies might be using older or less advanced technology, which can lead to frustrating interactions with their bots. So, while you might find yourself yelling "Just let me talk to a human!" more often than you'd like, remember that AI is still evolving. As the technology improves, so will the bots—and who knows, maybe in the future, they'll actually understand the difference between "I need help" and "I want to return a product"!

The way companies approach marketing and sales is also being transformed by AI. Businesses can use AI to analyze customer data and predict consumer behavior, which allows them to tailor marketing efforts and boost sales. For instance, machine learning algorithms help platforms like *Google Ads* and *Facebook* deliver highly targeted ads to specific demographics. These platforms don't just show generic ads; they analyze users' online activities and preferences to present content they're most likely to engage with. This means more effective advertising, with a higher chance of conversion, while reducing wasted ad spend. Similarly, AI-powered systems are now able to dynamically optimize pricing, taking into account market trends, competitor prices, and demand to maximize profits and minimize losses.

The supply chain and logistics industries have also seen massive improvements thanks to AI. Large companies like *Amazon* and *Walmart* use AI to predict product demand, which helps ensure their warehouses are stocked with the right goods at the right time. This predictive capability also helps improve the efficiency of delivery routes. AI algorithms can calculate the fastest and most cost-effective delivery options, reducing shipping costs and improving customer satisfaction. Additionally, the use of autonomous vehicles, including drones and self-driving trucks, is becoming more common. These AI-powered vehicles are capable of transporting goods more quickly and reliably, further cutting down on logistics costs and human error.

In healthcare, AI is changing the way doctors diagnose and treat patients. AI tools can analyze medical data, such as X-rays, MRIs, and CT scans, with incredible precision, often detecting problems that might be missed by the human eye. For example, *DeepMind*, a company owned by Google, has developed AI that can identify signs of eye disease and even predict the onset of conditions like kidney failure. This can be a game-changer for early diagnosis and treatment, potentially saving lives by catching diseases in their earliest, most treatable stages. In fact, AI is already being used to improve patient outcomes by providing doctors with real-time data and insights, allowing for more informed decisions. AI is also being employed in drug discovery, helping researchers identify potential treatments more quickly than traditional methods ever could.

AI IN EVERYDAY LIFE: HOW YOU CAN BENEFIT FROM AI RIGHT NOW

While AI is often associated with big businesses, it's not just something for corporations to play with—it's also something that can improve your everyday life. Whether you're using a voice assistant, streaming your favorite music, or getting personalized recommendations from your favorite shopping sites, AI is all around us, making things more convenient and efficient.

If you've ever interacted with a voice assistant like *Siri*, *Alexa*, or *Google Assistant*, you've already used AI. These assistants can help with all sorts of tasks, from setting alarms and reminders to providing weather updates, controlling smart home devices, or answering general knowledge questions. Over time, these assistants learn from your habits and preferences, which means they can offer more personalized help the longer you use them. For example, if you ask Alexa to play your favorite songs every morning, it will start playing them automatically without needing to be reminded. These devices may seem simple on the surface, but they're powered by complex AI algorithms that continuously evolve and improve.

But again, as with chatbots, these voice assistants aren't always perfect. They can be a little... let's say, "overly enthusiastic" sometimes. Ask *Siri* to "remind me about that meeting" and next thing you know, it's asking, "Which meeting? And would you like me to order coffee for you too?" It's as if *Siri* has its own idea of what your day should look like! But much like chatbots, voice assistants are getting smarter with every interaction, and these little quirks should be seen as part of the fun ride as AI continues to evolve.

One area where AI truly shines is in entertainment. If you've ever been on *Netflix*, *YouTube*, or *Spotify*, you've probably noticed how these platforms seem to know exactly what you want to watch or listen to. This is because AI is used to personalize recommendations based on your viewing or listening history. For instance, *Netflix* uses AI algorithms to recommend shows and movies that match your interests, while *Spotify* generates personalized playlists like *Discover Weekly*, filled with new songs you might enjoy. This type of AI is all about tailoring the experience to you, making your time spent on these platforms more enjoyable and efficient.

Another place where AI is making a difference is in smart homes. AI is embedded in devices like *Nest* thermostats, which learn your temperature preferences over time, and *Ring* doorbells, which use facial recognition to identify visitors. With smart devices like these, AI is helping to automate tasks around the house, making it easier to manage things like energy usage and security. AI-powered cameras can even monitor your home while you're away, alerting you if there's any unusual activity. With more connected devices entering the market, our homes are becoming smarter, safer, and more energy-efficient.

AI is also increasingly being used to help with health and fitness. Wearable devices like *Fitbit* and *Apple Watch* use AI to monitor your physical activity, heart rate, and even your sleep patterns. Over time, these devices can provide personalized recommendations to help you reach your fitness goals, whether that's improving your cardiovascular health or getting more rest. AI is also being used to track mental health, with apps like *Woebot* providing cognitive behavioral therapy through AI chatbots, offering support to people dealing with anxiety or depression.

AI IN THE WORKPLACE: INCREASING EFFICIENCY AND INNOVATION

As AI becomes more advanced, it's also revolutionizing how we work. Whether you're a small business owner or working a traditional office job, AI can boost your efficiency, reduce manual tasks, and even spark new ideas.

In the workplace, AI can handle routine tasks, freeing up employees to focus on more important and creative work. For example, if you're managing emails, an AI tool like *Grammarly* can automatically check for spelling and grammar mistakes, saving you time on editing. If you're scheduling meetings, AI-powered tools like *Clara* or *x.ai* can handle scheduling and send out invitations based on your availability. These types of tools are designed to make your life easier, allowing you to focus on the more strategic or creative parts of your job.

AI is also helping companies innovate by providing insights that might not be immediately obvious to humans. For instance, data analytics platforms like *Tableau* and *Power BI* use AI to uncover trends in large datasets, helping businesses make smarter, more informed decisions. In marketing, AI is used to analyze consumer behavior and develop targeted campaigns that are more likely to resonate with specific audiences. In finance, AI-powered algorithms are used to identify investment opportunities and predict market movements.

While these advancements are exciting, they also raise important questions. As AI takes over more tasks, what does that mean for jobs? Some fear that AI will make certain positions obsolete, but the truth is, AI is just as likely to create new jobs as it is to eliminate old ones. It's also opening the door to entirely new industries that didn't exist before, offering new opportunities for innovation and entrepreneurship.

LOOKING FORWARD: THE FUTURE OF AI

So, where is all this going? What's next for AI?

If we've learned anything so far, it's that AI is only getting started. Whether it's improving customer service, enhancing entertainment experiences, or transforming industries like healthcare and finance, the possibilities seem endless. And as AI continues to evolve, it's likely that we'll see even more groundbreaking advancements in the years to come.

Sure, chatbots might still get a little confused sometimes, and your voice assistant may have a few "overenthusiastic" moments. But that's all part of the charm. The reality is, AI is here to stay, and it's already shaping the future of work, entertainment, and everyday life in ways we never imagined. Whether you're excited or slightly intimidated by all this change, one thing's for sure: we're all in for one wild ride as AI continues to evolve and transform the world around us.

03

THE POWER BEHIND AI – DEEP LEARNING AND NEURAL NETWORKS

AI has made incredible strides over the past decade, but the real breakthrough that's driving most of today's AI advancements is deep learning. Deep learning, a subset of machine learning, is at the heart of everything from image recognition to language translation and self-driving cars. If AI were a car, deep learning would be the engine under the hood, making everything run smoother, faster, and more efficiently.

UNDERSTANDING DEEP LEARNING

To get a better understanding of deep learning, let's take a step back and look at how traditional machine learning works. Machine learning involves training algorithms to recognize patterns in data. For example, a machine learning model might be trained to recognize pictures of cats by being shown thousands of images labeled as "cat" or "not cat." Over time, the model learns to identify the features of a cat—pointy ears, whiskers, and so on—until it can spot a cat in an image it's never seen before.

While traditional machine learning is powerful, it can only go so far. This is where deep learning takes things to the next level. Deep learning is inspired by how the human brain works. It uses structures called artificial neural networks, which are composed of layers of nodes, or "neurons," that process information in a hierarchical manner. Essentially, deep learning mimics how our brains process and understand the world, allowing it to tackle much more complex problems.

In a deep learning model, each layer of the network is responsible for learning specific features of the data. In the case of image recognition, the first layer might focus on simple things like edges and shapes, while later layers will pick up more complex patterns, like eyes, noses, and eventually, the whole cat! The more layers a network has, the more complex features it can learn to recognize, allowing it to make highly accurate predictions and decisions.

THE RISE OF NEURAL NETWORKS

Neural networks were actually first developed in the 1950s and 1960s, but for decades, they didn't live up to their potential. Computing power was too limited, and data was hard to come by. It wasn't until the early 2000s, when powerful GPUs (graphic processing units) became more widely available, that deep learning really began to take off. The combination of better hardware and vast amounts of data has allowed neural networks to perform tasks that were once thought to be the domain of human intelligence.

The breakthroughs in deep learning are largely thanks to a few key pioneers. One of the most influential is *Geoffrey Hinton*, a British-Canadian computer scientist often referred to as the "godfather of deep learning." Hinton's work in the 1980s and 1990s helped lay the foundation for modern deep learning, particularly his development of the backpropagation algorithm, which allows neural networks to learn from their mistakes and improve over time. Alongside *Yann LeCun* and *Yoshua Bengio*, Hinton was awarded the 2018 Turing Award for his work in neural networks, marking a turning point for AI research.

The work of these pioneers has had a profound impact, enabling AI systems to recognize images, understand speech, and process natural language with incredible accuracy. But as powerful as deep learning is, it's still evolving—and researchers continue to make breakthroughs that improve its capabilities every year.

AI AND NATURAL LANGUAGE PROCESSING (NLP)

One of the most exciting areas of deep learning is in natural language processing (NLP), which focuses on teaching computers to understand, interpret, and generate human language. NLP is the technology behind many AI systems you're familiar with, like virtual assistants (*Siri*, *Alexa*, *Google Assistant*) and chatbots. It's also the technology that powers advanced AI models like *OpenAI's GPT* series (which includes ChatGPT) and *Google's BERT*.

For example, GPT (Generative Pretrained Transformer) is based on deep learning and has been trained on a vast amount of text data to generate human-like text. This allows it to understand the context of a conversation, generate responses, and even write essays or stories on its own. It's the same technology behind ChatGPT, which you've probably interacted with to ask questions or get help with tasks. The level of understanding and fluency in conversation that these models can achieve is unprecedented, and it's all thanks to deep learning.

But NLP doesn't stop at just chatting with computers. It's also playing a huge role in translation, sentiment analysis, and even healthcare. For example, AI systems trained on NLP techniques can now analyze medical records to identify patterns that might indicate health risks, helping doctors make earlier diagnoses. *IBM Watson Health* has even used NLP to sift through large volumes of clinical data, making it easier for healthcare professionals to stay up to date with the latest research and provide better care for their patients.

REINFORCEMENT LEARNING: TEACHING AI TO LEARN BY DOING

Another crucial aspect of deep learning is reinforcement learning, which is the type of machine learning used in AI systems that learn by interacting with their environment. Unlike supervised learning, where models are trained on labeled data, reinforcement learning is all about trial and error. The AI is given a goal, and through experimentation, it learns what actions will get it closer to that goal. Over time, the system gets better and better at achieving its objectives.

Reinforcement learning is behind many of AI's most impressive feats. For instance, *DeepMind*'s *AlphaGo*, which famously defeated world champion Go players in 2016, used reinforcement learning to master the game. The system played millions of rounds against itself, learning from its mistakes and eventually becoming one of the best Go players in the world. Similarly, reinforcement learning is being used to train AI systems to play video games, optimize supply chains, and even control robots.

But reinforcement learning isn't without its challenges. It requires massive amounts of data and computational power to train the systems, and there's always the risk of unintended consequences—especially if the AI takes a shortcut or learns a strategy that's unexpected. That's why researchers are constantly working to improve reinforcement learning techniques and make them safer and more reliable.

AI AND CREATIVITY: MACHINES THAT THINK OUTSIDE THE BOX

AI isn't just about crunching numbers and solving problems—it's also being used to push the boundaries of creativity. Deep learning has been used to create everything from music and art to poetry and even recipes. While AI-created art might seem like something out of science fiction, it's actually becoming a reality.

OpenAI's DALL•E, for example, is an AI model that can generate images from textual descriptions. You could give DALL•E a prompt like "a futuristic city on Mars with flying cars," and it will create a completely unique image based on that description. This opens up exciting possibilities for artists, designers, and creators, offering them a new tool to bring their ideas to life. Similarly, AI-generated music, like *Amper Music*, is helping artists compose new songs and soundtracks by analyzing existing music and generating original compositions.

AI is also making strides in fields like fashion, where deep learning is being used to predict trends and design clothing. Companies like *Stitch Fix* use AI to analyze customer preferences and suggest clothing items that fit their individual style. It's a creative use of AI that helps businesses offer more personalized services to their customers while also pushing the envelope in terms of innovation.

LOOKING AHEAD: THE FUTURE OF DEEP LEARNING

As deep learning continues to evolve, it's likely that we'll see even more groundbreaking innovations in AI. From self-improving algorithms to systems that can generate their own ideas, the possibilities are endless. But while deep learning has come a long way, it's still just the beginning. Researchers are working on new architectures and methods that could revolutionize the field and open up entirely new areas of AI.

Whether it's in healthcare, entertainment, or autonomous driving, deep learning is already shaping the future. The next few years will likely bring even more advances, and the world will continue to be amazed by the power and potential of AI.

04

HOW AI IS USED IN BIG BUSINESS

AI IN THE BUSINESS WORLD: A GAME CHANGER

AI has moved from being a futuristic concept to an essential tool in business today. It's transforming industries, changing how companies operate, and shaping the future of customer interactions. It's not just about automating basic tasks—AI is enhancing decision-making, improving efficiency, and even creating entirely new ways of doing business. Let's take a look at how AI is making waves in various sectors, from self-driving cars to customer service and logistics.

SELF-DRIVING CARS: THE FUTURE IS NOW

One of the most talked-about uses of AI is in self-driving cars. Companies like *Tesla*, *Waymo* (part of *Alphabet*), and *Cruise* (a subsidiary of *General Motors*) are developing cars that can drive themselves without human input.

So, how does AI make a car drive itself? It's a combination of sensors, cameras, radar, and machine learning algorithms. The car constantly collects data about its surroundings and processes it using AI to make decisions—like when to stop at a red light, when to speed up, and how to navigate tricky traffic situations. Essentially, AI allows the car to "see" and "think" in real-time, making decisions that would normally require a human driver.

And it's not just U.S.-based companies pushing the boundaries. In China, *Baidu* is leading the way with its autonomous vehicle program, using AI to power self-driving taxis in select cities. *Didi Chuxing*, another Chinese company, is also working on AI-powered ridesharing vehicles. Meanwhile, *Volkswagen* and *BMW* in Germany are using AI to improve their own self-driving technology. The race for autonomous cars is truly global, with breakthroughs happening all over the world.

AI IN CUSTOMER SERVICE: MAKING INTERACTIONS SMOOTHER

We've already touched on the role AI plays in customer service, but let's go a bit deeper into how it's changing the way businesses interact with customers. Gone are the days of waiting on hold for hours to speak to a customer service representative. AI is stepping in to streamline this process, making it faster and more efficient.

Take *Bank of America* as an example. The bank's AI-powered assistant, *Erica*, helps customers with everything from checking account balances to scheduling appointments. What makes *Erica* so effective is its ability to learn and improve over time. The more customers interact with it, the better it gets at providing relevant answers and personalized recommendations. It's like having a helpful, always-available assistant at your fingertips.

Another great example is *Sephora*, which uses AI to create personalized shopping experiences. Through its *Sephora Virtual Artist* app, customers can try on makeup virtually using augmented reality (AR) powered by AI. The app analyzes the customer's facial features and suggests products that suit their skin tone, all while giving them a fun, interactive experience.

However, it's important to remember that chatbots, as efficient as they are, are still not perfect. While *Erica* and *Sephora*'s Virtual Artist can handle many tasks, they still have limitations, especially when dealing with complex issues. Have you ever tried to explain a more complicated problem to a chatbot that just keeps offering you the same basic responses? It can be frustrating! But the good news is, AI is constantly improving, so these systems are getting better every day. The key takeaway here is that AI is helping businesses provide quicker, more personalized service, and it's only going to get better.

AI IN SUPPLY CHAIN AND LOGISTICS: SMARTER, FASTER, CHEAPER

AI is having a big impact on the way products move around the world. Companies in logistics are using AI to optimize their supply chains, making them more efficient and less costly. For example, *Amazon* uses AI to predict what customers are likely to buy and when, allowing it to stock the right products in its warehouses. By analyzing historical data and customer buying patterns, Amazon's AI-driven system can forecast demand and make sure that items are available when customers need them, cutting down on shipping delays and reducing excess inventory.

In China, *Alibaba* is using AI to optimize its logistics network. Its AI-powered platform tracks every package in real time, helping the company predict when it will arrive and ensuring it takes the fastest route possible. This not only speeds up delivery times but also cuts down on energy use, making it a win-win for both the company and the environment.

Not to be outdone, European companies like *DHL* are also harnessing AI to predict delivery times and monitor inventory. By using AI-powered robots to pick and pack items, *DHL* can speed up its operations and improve accuracy. The AI even helps the company predict which routes will be the most efficient, reducing fuel consumption and carbon emissions in the process.

AI IN MARKETING: PERSONALIZED EXPERIENCES ACROSS THE GLOBE

In the world of marketing, AI is enabling businesses to create highly personalized experiences for their customers. It's no longer about sending out mass emails or using blanket marketing tactics. With AI, companies can target their audience with tailored content based on individual preferences and behaviors.

Take *Netflix* as an example. Every time you watch a show or movie, Netflix's AI-powered recommendation engine learns more about your preferences, offering up suggestions that are likely to match your tastes. This personalized experience keeps users engaged and makes them more likely to stick with the service.

Similarly, *Spotify* uses AI to create personalized playlists for its users. By analyzing listening habits, Spotify's AI can suggest new songs that align with a person's tastes. AI in marketing isn't just about convenience—it's about building stronger connections with customers.

And it's not just U.S. companies leading the charge. In India, *Flipkart*—one of the largest e-commerce platforms in the country—is using AI to personalize shopping experiences. By analyzing consumer behavior, *Flipkart* is able to recommend products to customers in real time, boosting engagement and sales. And over in China, *Alibaba* is using AI to deliver personalized ads and product recommendations, enhancing the shopping experience for users while also improving sales conversion rates.

AI IN FINANCE: PREDICTING THE FUTURE

The financial sector is another area where AI is making significant strides. From fraud detection to stock market predictions, AI is helping financial institutions make smarter decisions, faster.

For example, many investment firms use AI-powered algorithms to analyze massive amounts of data and predict market trends. These systems can process information much faster than human traders, allowing them to identify patterns that would be hard for a person to spot. *Robo-advisors*, like those offered by *Betterment* and *Wealthfront*, are another AI application in the finance world. These platforms use AI to help users manage their investments, offering personalized recommendations based on factors like risk tolerance, investment goals, and market conditions.

In addition to improving decision-making, AI is also playing a key role in fraud detection. Banks and credit card companies use AI to analyze transaction data in real time, identifying suspicious activity and flagging potential fraud. By analyzing patterns in spending behavior, AI can spot anomalies that might indicate fraudulent transactions, allowing companies to take action before things escalate.

THE GLOBAL LANDSCAPE OF AI: IT'S HAPPENING EVERYWHERE

While many of the companies we've highlighted so far are based in the U.S., AI is a truly global phenomenon. Countries around the world are investing heavily in AI, seeing it as a key to future economic growth and innovation.

For example, *DeepMind*—a British AI research lab that was acquired by *Google*—is making big strides in healthcare. One of the lab's key breakthroughs has been in the early detection of diseases, like eye conditions and cancer. Their AI system can analyze medical images, such as retinal scans, to detect early signs of diseases that might otherwise go unnoticed by human doctors. In some cases, AI has been shown to be even more accurate than human doctors in diagnosing certain conditions, which could ultimately save lives.

Meanwhile, *Samsung* in South Korea is using AI to enhance its products. One area where AI is making an impact is in the development of smart appliances, such as refrigerators, washing machines, and air conditioners. By using AI to understand user habits, *Samsung*'s smart appliances can adjust their settings for greater energy efficiency. For example, a smart fridge might suggest recipes based on what's inside, while a washing machine could recommend the best wash cycle for your laundry, saving both time and energy.

In China, *Alibaba* is using AI to power its e-commerce platform, allowing it to recommend products to customers in real time. But *Alibaba* is also looking to the skies—literally. The company has been experimenting with AI-powered drones for delivery, cutting down delivery times and costs while offering an innovative, high-tech solution to logistics challenges.

AI's global impact is undeniable, and it's clear that different countries and companies are approaching it in unique ways. Whether it's in healthcare, retail, or transportation, AI is driving innovation across the globe, and it's exciting to think about what the future holds.

CHAPTER

05

AI IN EVERYDAY LIFE –
YOUR PHONE, YOUR HOME,
AND BEYOND

AI isn't just something that tech experts and futuristic movies talk about anymore. It's slowly but surely becoming part of your daily routine, whether you're realizing it or not. From smartphones and home devices to personalized online experiences, AI is reshaping how we interact with the world around us. Let's dive into how these technological marvels are working their magic behind the scenes to make life easier, faster, and a bit more fun.

AI IN YOUR SMARTPHONE: MORE THAN JUST A CALL AND TEXT MACHINE

If you take a quick look at your smartphone, you might just think it's a device for browsing the web, chatting with friends, or binge-watching the latest series. But what you might not realize is that your phone is essentially a mini AI powerhouse, doing all kinds of cool things to improve your day-to-day activities.

First, there's the voice assistant. Whether it's *Siri*, *Google Assistant*, or *Alexa*, these AI-driven tools are helping you do everything from setting reminders to finding the nearest coffee shop, all through a simple voice command. With the magic of natural language processing (NLP), these assistants are designed to understand your tone, language, and even your quirky requests (like asking *Siri* to tell you a joke). Thanks to deep learning, voice assistants can handle more complex tasks and become more accurate over time, learning from past interactions.

Then there's facial recognition technology—another AI marvel that's found its way onto smartphones. With the tap of your face, your phone unlocks. The technology maps out your unique facial features and checks if they match the stored data. It's a sleek, secure, and (let's face it) futuristic way to protect your personal device. And AI doesn't stop there. It analyzes the lighting, angles, and even your facial expressions to ensure accurate recognition, no matter the time of day.

Of course, it's not just about keeping your device secure. AI is also behind the apps that give you personalized recommendations, making your life that much easier. Platforms like *Netflix* and *Spotify* use AI to figure out what you like based on past behavior and recommend your next binge-worthy series or playlist. Online shopping apps, like *Amazon*, use the same algorithms to suggest products you might want, based on everything from your purchase history to your browsing patterns.

AI AT HOME: MAKING YOUR LIVING SPACE SMARTER

But wait—AI isn't just sitting in your phone. It's creeping into your home as well. And it's making everything from lighting to security more convenient and efficient.

Think about your smart home devices. With a *Google Home*, *Amazon Echo*, or *Apple HomePod*, you can control almost everything in your house with your voice: the lights, the thermostat, the music, and even your coffee machine (if you're lucky). These devices, powered by AI, use natural language processing to understand your commands and respond accordingly. So when you say, "Hey *Google*, turn off the lights," your AI assistant knows exactly what you mean.

And it's not just about convenience—it's about safety too. AI is helping to keep your home secure. Smart security cameras, for example, use machine learning algorithms to detect unusual patterns of activity. If someone unfamiliar is lurking outside your door, these cameras can flag it and alert you in real-time. Companies like *Ring* use this AI-powered technology to analyze faces and objects in your camera's range, making sure your security system gets smarter the longer you use it.

And don't forget your smart thermostats, like *Nest*. These devices use AI to learn your preferences over time, adjusting the temperature based on when you're home or even your mood (okay, maybe not your mood—yet!). But the more you interact with them, the more efficient they become, helping save energy and keeping you comfortable.

PERSONALIZED SHOPPING AND RECOMMENDATIONS

It's no surprise that AI has made its way into shopping. In fact, it's become a game-changer for how businesses understand what you want. Take *Amazon*—its AI algorithms not only suggest products based on your past purchases but also on what people similar to you have bought. This is the power of machine learning in action: by analyzing tons of data, AI helps companies predict what you're likely to buy before you even know you need it.

Social media platforms like *Facebook* and *Instagram* also use AI to curate your feed. By learning from your activity—what you like, comment on, or share—these platforms serve up more of the content that interests you, all in an attempt to keep you scrolling. The more you interact, the more personalized your experience becomes.

And then there's AI in online retail. Brands like *Sephora* are using virtual assistants and AI-powered tools to provide personalized shopping experiences. The beauty retailer's *Virtual Artist* app lets you try on makeup virtually, using AI to analyze your face and suggest shades that will suit you. Pretty cool, right? This AI magic doesn't just help you shop; it makes the whole experience a lot more fun, too.

BANKING WITH AI: FROM SIMPLE TRANSACTIONS TO FINANCIAL INSIGHTS

AI has also found its way into banking. *Bank of America's* virtual assistant, *Erica*, uses AI to handle customer inquiries, track spending, and even give financial advice. Erica can remind you when bills are due, suggest ways to save money, and even forecast your spending habits. It's like having your own personal banker, available 24/7. And it doesn't stop there: AI is making banking faster and more secure. Fraud detection systems powered by AI can instantly analyze transactions and spot suspicious activities, alerting banks to potential security risks before they even have a chance to escalate.

THE AI-POWERED FUTURE OF HEALTHCARE

AI is also improving healthcare, and it's not just about robots in surgery. AI-driven systems are helping doctors diagnose diseases more accurately and quickly than ever before. *Siemens Healthineers* offers advanced imaging solutions that use machine learning to help identify early signs of conditions like cancer and heart disease. These AI-powered tools can analyze medical images—think X-rays, MRIs, and CT scans—more quickly than a human could, spotting patterns and abnormalities that might be missed by the naked eye. By catching these issues early, doctors can start treatments sooner, improving patient outcomes.

DeepMind, an AI company owned by *Google*, is making waves in healthcare as well. Their algorithms are used to diagnose eye conditions, like diabetic retinopathy, by analyzing retinal scans. The AI system can detect early signs of the disease, even before it causes symptoms, allowing doctors to intervene early and prevent blindness. This isn't just theory—it's happening now.

06

AI FOR YOU – MAKING ARTIFICIAL INTELLIGENCE WORK FOR YOU

Artificial intelligence is no longer confined to laboratories or billion-dollar corporations; it's become an integral part of how we live and work. This section explores how AI can boost your efficiency, transform industries, and introduce you to the different types of AI shaping our world.

Boosting Your Efficiency

Managing our ever-growing to-do lists can feel like a juggling act, but AI is here to lend a hand. From automating mundane tasks to supercharging your productivity, the tools available today cater to both office workers and remote professionals.

AI AT WORK: YOUR VIRTUAL ASSISTANT

AI tools like Microsoft Copilot, Notion, and Slack's AI integrations have become invaluable for automating workflows. These programs can summarize lengthy emails, organize project timelines, or even suggest edits for documents. For instance, Microsoft Copilot analyzes spreadsheets in moments, providing actionable insights on financial trends.

For remote professionals, apps like Otter.ai transcribe meetings in real-time, and AI-powered calendar assistants like Clockwise optimize your schedule to minimize back-to-back meetings and preserve focus time.

Humorous Note:

Of course, AI isn't immune to hiccups—imagine asking it to "schedule a meeting with the design team" and having it book lunch with your dentist instead!

AI FOR PERSONAL PRODUCTIVITY

Personal life benefits too. Tools like Todoist use AI to prioritize tasks, while apps like Grammarly ensure your emails and reports sound professional. Even routine errands, like shopping lists, are streamlined by voice assistants like Alexa, which can predict what you're running low on.

AI doesn't just save time; it also reduces cognitive load, leaving you free to focus on what truly matters—whether that's work deadlines or family time.

EXPLORING AI BY INDUSTRY

AI's versatility means it's revolutionizing multiple industries simultaneously. From healthcare and education to agriculture and finance, the transformative potential of AI is profound.

Healthcare: Diagnosing and Healing

AI is making healthcare faster, more accurate, and more accessible. In radiology, AI systems like Google's DeepMind analyze scans to detect early signs of diseases such as cancer or diabetic retinopathy. These systems don't replace doctors but act as second pairs of eyes, spotting patterns that might otherwise go unnoticed.

In hospitals, AI-driven chatbots guide patients to the appropriate departments, and wearable devices like Apple Watches monitor heart rates, flagging irregularities that could signal cardiac events.

Finance: Smarter Money Management

Banks and investment firms use AI to analyze market trends, detect fraudulent activities, and personalize financial advice. Robo-advisors like Betterment create customized investment strategies based on an individual's risk tolerance and goals.

Fun Fact: Some AI tools even help you negotiate bills! Apps like Trim identify unnecessary subscriptions and negotiate better rates with service providers.

Education: Personalized Learning

AI is a game-changer for education. Platforms like Khan Academy now include AI tutors that adapt lessons to individual learning styles, ensuring every student progresses at their own pace. Similarly, AI tools help teachers by grading assignments and identifying areas where students struggle.

Agriculture: Feeding the Future

AI is addressing global food challenges by optimizing farming techniques. Tools like John Deere's precision farming systems use AI to analyze soil conditions, recommend planting patterns, and even deploy autonomous tractors.

TYPES OF AI YOU SHOULD KNOW

AI comes in many flavors, each designed for specific tasks. Here's a breakdown of the most common types and what they're good for:

Written AI

AI-powered writing tools like ChatGPT and Jasper can generate blog posts, marketing content, and even poetry. Writers often use these tools to brainstorm ideas or polish drafts.

Example: In journalism, AI platforms like Wordsmith generate real-time financial reports and sports summaries, freeing reporters to focus on investigative work.

Visual AI

Visual AI includes image recognition software and creative tools. Adobe's Firefly, for instance, allows users to generate stunning graphics by typing simple descriptions. Meanwhile, apps like Google Lens can identify objects in photos or translate text from images on the go.

Practical Tip:

If you're a budding photographer, AI tools like Skylum Luminar can enhance your photos by automatically adjusting lighting and removing blemishes.

Generative AI for Music and Video

Music producers are embracing tools like Amper Music, which lets anyone create royalty-free tracks by setting tempo and mood preferences. Similarly, platforms like Runway ML enable filmmakers to produce Hollywood-grade special effects without the need for a full studio.

How Does It Work?

At their core, these systems rely on deep learning—an advanced form of machine learning that mimics human neural networks. By processing vast amounts of data, these models "learn" to recognize patterns, generate content, and make predictions.

07

THE TOOLS OF AI

AI isn't just a buzzword anymore—it's become a set of practical tools that anyone can use. In this section, we'll explore some of the most popular AI applications available today, diving into how they work and what they can do. We'll also take a closer look at ChatGPT, Grok, and their competitors, as well as compare the strengths of AI tools against traditional search engines like Google.

AI APPLICATIONS YOU CAN USE TODAY

AI tools are transforming how we work, create, and interact with the world. Whether you're an artist, a coder, or someone who just needs to write an email faster, there's an AI tool out there for you.

Writing Tools

Writing apps like ChatGPT, Jasper, and Writesonic help you generate text, from blog posts to short stories. They use large language models trained on billions of data points to predict and create coherent, relevant text based on your input.

For example, ChatGPT allows users to draft essays, while Jasper is tailored for marketing copy, helping businesses create persuasive product descriptions or ads. These tools save time but also inspire creativity by offering fresh perspectives.

Humorous Note:

They might occasionally "hallucinate" facts or invent wildly inaccurate claims. Imagine writing, "Tell me about penguins," and getting, "Penguins were the first animals to land on the moon!"

Art and Design

Tools like MidJourney, Adobe Firefly, and DALL·E 2 generate stunning visuals. You provide a description—say, "a futuristic city at sunset with flying cars"—and these platforms create images that could rival professional artists.

Meanwhile, Canva's AI integrations let users generate custom layouts and enhance photos with minimal effort, making graphic design accessible to anyone.

Coding Assistants

GitHub Copilot is a boon for developers, writing snippets of code or even entire functions based on natural language descriptions. For budding programmers, it's like having a senior developer sitting beside you, correcting syntax errors and optimizing logic.

Real-world Use: A small business owner with no coding experience can use Copilot to create a simple e-commerce site.

Music and Video Creation

AI tools like Amper Music and AIVA let non-musicians compose tracks for podcasts or videos by simply selecting a genre or mood. For video creators, platforms like Runway ML automate editing, enhance visuals, and even create unique special effects.

AI in Everyday Life

From AI-powered fitness apps like MyFitnessPal, which analyze dietary patterns, to language learning apps like Duolingo, AI tools integrate seamlessly into daily routines. Voice assistants like Siri and Alexa have become household staples, answering questions and managing smart homes.

CHATGPT VS. GOOGLE: A TALE OF TWO TITANS

ChatGPT and Google serve different purposes, but they're often compared due to their ability to provide information.

ChatGPT: Your Conversational Partner

Unlike Google, ChatGPT generates coherent, contextually relevant responses in conversational language. It's perfect for brainstorming ideas, learning about complex topics, or even writing that tricky opening line for an email.

Example: Ask ChatGPT, "How can I explain quantum physics to a 10-year-old?" It'll break down the concept into digestible pieces, making it easier to understand.

However, ChatGPT has its limits. Its responses depend on the quality of the input and the data it was trained on, which means it might not always have the most up-to-date or accurate information.

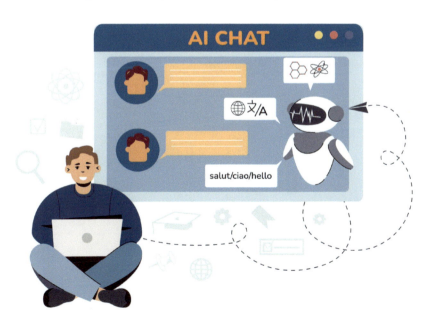

Google: The King of Search

Google excels at delivering vast amounts of data quickly. It's the go-to for specific answers, like finding the capital of a country or checking the weather forecast. Its ability to scour the internet and rank results by relevance makes it unparalleled for research.

Where it falls short is in generating nuanced, creative responses. For instance, Google might show you articles on writing a business pitch, but ChatGPT will help you draft the pitch itself.

CHATGPT VS. GOOGLE: PUT IT TO THE TEST

Now that we've compared ChatGPT and Google, let's turn theory into practice. This isn't just about reading—it's time to get hands-on and see the difference for yourself. Below are a few challenges you can try out using both tools. By the end, you'll better understand when to reach for Google and when ChatGPT is the better choice.

Challenge 1: Crafting a Creative Story

Your Task:
Ask both ChatGPT and Google for help creating a short story.

Example Prompt for ChatGPT:
"Write me a short story about a dog who saves its owner during a snowstorm."

Example Search for Google:
"Short story about a dog saving its owner in a snowstorm."

What to Look For:

- 🌐 **ChatGPT** will generate a custom, original story tailored to your request. You can even refine it further by asking, "Make the dog a golden retriever," or "Add a twist ending."

- 🌐 **Google** will return links to existing stories, articles, or writing resources. You'll have to sift through them to find something close to what you imagined, but it won't create anything personalized.

Challenge 2: Personal Productivity Hack

Your Task:

Ask both tools for ways to manage your daily schedule as a working parent juggling kids and remote work.

Example Prompt for ChatGPT:

"Create a daily schedule for a remote-working parent with two kids, including time for meals, work, and breaks."

Example Search for Google:

"Daily schedule for a remote-working parent."

What to Look For:

- 🌐 **ChatGPT** will craft a detailed and customized schedule, potentially including advice on time-blocking or when to fit in self-care.

- 🌐 **Google** will link to blogs or parenting websites. While useful, you'll need to pull ideas from multiple sources and adapt them yourself.

Challenge 3: Understanding a Complex Topic

Your Task:

Ask both tools to explain a tricky concept in simple terms.

Example Prompt for ChatGPT:

"Explain the concept of black holes in a way a 10-year-old could understand."

Example Search for Google:

"Black holes explained simply."

What to Look For:

- **ChatGPT** will provide an engaging, easy-to-understand explanation that adapts to the tone you set. If the first explanation doesn't click, ask, "Make it simpler" or "Use a fun analogy."

- **Google** will return articles and videos, which might be highly scientific or inconsistent in quality.

Challenge 4: Getting Cooking Inspiration

Your Task:

Ask for help with dinner ideas using specific ingredients.

Example Prompt for ChatGPT:

"I have chicken, broccoli, and rice. What can I cook for dinner?"

Example Search for Google:

"Recipes with chicken, broccoli, and rice."

What to Look For:

- **ChatGPT** will act like your personal chef, suggesting creative ways to combine your ingredients and even walking you through cooking instructions step-by-step.

- **Google** will provide links to recipes, but you'll have to sort through options, some of which might require ingredients you don't have.

Challenge 5: Getting Feedback on a Draft

Your Task:

Test out both tools for editing and feedback.

Example Prompt for ChatGPT:

"Here's my draft for an email to my boss about taking time off next week. Can you make it more professional?"

Example Search for Google:

"How to write an email to your boss about taking time off."

What to Look For:

- **ChatGPT** will rewrite your email, offering a polished version that's ready to send. If it doesn't feel quite right, ask, "Make it sound more casual," or "Use friendlier language."

- **Google** will show you templates or general advice, but it won't directly improve your specific draft.

TAKEAWAY FROM THE CHALLENGES

While Google is a treasure trove of information, it relies on you to filter, interpret, and adapt the content. ChatGPT, on the other hand, works with you to create, refine, and personalize outputs. By trying these challenges, you'll experience firsthand how ChatGPT can provide more tailored, granular results.

So, give it a go—and remember, if you're not happy with the first answer ChatGPT gives, ask it to try again! Sometimes the magic is in the back-and-forth conversation.

The Verdict

These tools aren't in competition—they're complementary. Use Google for fact-checking and broad searches, and turn to ChatGPT when you need creativity or context.

CATEGORIZED RECOMMENDATIONS FOR AI APPLICATIONS

To help you make the most of AI, here's a quick guide to some standout tools across various domains:

Writing and Content Creation

- 🌐 **ChatGPT**: General-purpose writing and brainstorming.
- 🌐 **Jasper**: Marketing copy and ad creation.
- 🌐 **Writesonic**: Social media posts, headlines, and emails.

Visual Design and Creativity

- **Adobe Firefly**: Stunning graphic creation with simple text prompts.
- **DALL·E 2**: Image generation based on detailed descriptions.
- **Canva**: Easy design with AI-assisted templates.

Coding and Development

- **GitHub Copilot**: Assists with writing and debugging code.
- **Replit Ghostwriter**: For real-time coding suggestions and error corrections.

Music and Video Production

- **Runway ML**: Simplifies video editing and visual effects.
- **AIVA**: Composes original music tracks.
- **Amper Music**: Generates background scores for projects.

Personal Productivity

- **Notion AI**: Automates task organization and note-taking.
- **Clockwise**: Optimizes schedules for better time management.
- **Grammarly**: Enhances writing clarity and professionalism.

08

THE IMPACT OF AI ON WORK

AI isn't just a buzzword—it's actively transforming workplaces worldwide. It's automating repetitive tasks, helping workers make better decisions, and creating new roles that didn't exist a decade ago. But with change comes uncertainty, and for many, that raises an important question: *What does AI mean for my job?*

The truth is, AI is both a disruptor and an innovator. It's eliminating some roles, particularly those based on routine tasks, but it's also opening the door to entirely new opportunities. To understand its impact, let's explore how AI is reshaping the job market and redefining work as we know it.

JOBS AI IS REPLACING

As AI continues to evolve, its impact on the job market is undeniable. Some jobs are already being automated, while others are predicted to be phased out over the next few decades. But how exactly is AI replacing jobs, and what does this mean for the workers currently in those roles?

First, let's talk about some of the roles that are already being replaced by AI. In many industries, repetitive, manual, or data-heavy tasks are being handled more efficiently by AI systems. For example, in manufacturing, robots have long been taking on assembly line jobs. Today, these robots are more advanced, capable of tasks such as inspection, quality control, and even certain aspects of packaging, reducing the need for human workers in those areas. According to the World Economic Forum, automation could replace 85 million jobs worldwide by 2025, particularly in sectors like manufacturing, transportation, and customer service.

One high-profile area where AI is taking jobs is customer service. Many companies, from banks to retail giants, have implemented AI-powered chatbots to handle routine inquiries. These bots are designed to answer customer questions, process transactions, and even resolve issues that previously required a human representative. While chatbots like those used by Bank of America or Sephora are still limited in their ability to understand complex issues, their ability to address basic queries is making human customer service roles redundant for simpler tasks.

Then there's the rise of autonomous vehicles. Self-driving technology, which relies heavily on AI, is set to transform the transportation industry. While companies like Tesla, Google's Waymo, and Uber are leading the way in autonomous vehicle development, many truck drivers, delivery drivers, and taxi drivers are facing the potential loss of their jobs. In fact, a report from the McKinsey Global Institute estimates that by 2030, up to 15 million American workers could be displaced by automation, with truck drivers being one of the most vulnerable groups.

AI is also making inroads into more professional and white-collar jobs. In the legal profession, for example, AI is already being used to automate document review and contract analysis—tasks that once required hours of human labor. AI tools like Ross Intelligence use natural language processing to help lawyers quickly analyze large volumes of legal texts. While these systems are still in their infancy, they have the potential to drastically reduce the number of junior lawyers and paralegals needed for research-heavy tasks.

Some prominent figures, like Elon Musk, have warned about the speed at which automation could take over jobs. Musk has repeatedly stated that AI and automation will inevitably cause massive disruption in the labor market, and the workforce needs to be prepared for it. He's advocated for universal basic income (UBI) as a solution, where citizens are provided with a guaranteed income to offset job loss caused by AI.

However, while AI is poised to replace many jobs, it's important to recognize that this isn't the end of work—it's simply a shift. Many jobs will evolve, and new roles will emerge to support the growing presence of AI.

JOBS AI WILL CREATE

While it's true that AI will replace some jobs, it will also create entirely new ones. As AI technology advances, industries will need new kinds of expertise, and new professions will emerge to support this AI-powered future. The rise of AI will lead to a transformation in the workforce, not a complete elimination of work.

One of the most obvious areas where AI is creating jobs is in AI research and development itself. As AI continues to grow, there will be an increasing demand for professionals with skills in machine learning, natural language processing, and robotics. In fact, according to a 2020 report by the World Economic Forum, AI specialists are already among the most in-demand roles. Companies like Google, Microsoft, and Amazon are hiring AI and machine learning engineers at a rapid pace, pushing the need for more educational programs to train the next generation of AI experts.

The healthcare industry is another area where AI will create new opportunities. As AI becomes more integrated into medical practices, professionals will be needed to work alongside AI systems, interpret their results, and ensure their correct application in patient care. For example, AI can analyze medical images and detect abnormalities such as tumors with greater accuracy than human doctors in some cases. But while AI can assist in diagnosis, the human touch will still be necessary for final decisions and patient care. The need for data analysts, AI specialists in healthcare, and medical professionals who understand AI will only increase.

Another sector benefiting from AI's rise is the entertainment industry. As AI becomes more capable of generating art, music, and even video, creative professionals will have new tools to enhance their work. Graphic designers, video editors, and musicians will collaborate with AI to create content more efficiently. For example, AI tools like OpenAI's Jukedeck are being used to create royalty-free music, while AI-powered animation programs are changing the way movies are made. These tools don't replace the artist, but instead, they augment creativity and provide new possibilities for storytelling and design.

The rise of autonomous systems, like self-driving cars and drones, is also leading to the creation of entirely new roles. For instance, drone operators and engineers are now in high demand as businesses experiment with using drones for deliveries, monitoring, and even entertainment. Similarly, autonomous vehicles will need specialized technicians who can maintain and troubleshoot AI-powered cars. Companies like Tesla and Waymo are already expanding their workforce to include these new roles.

There are also opportunities in the education sector, as AI systems are used to provide personalized learning experiences for students. Teachers and educational administrators will need to be equipped with the knowledge to integrate AI into the classroom and use it to tailor educational experiences to individual students' needs.

Prominent voices in the tech world, including Satya Nadella, CEO of Microsoft, have emphasized the potential for AI to create new jobs, particularly in areas like tech development and healthcare. Nadella has even suggested that as AI continues to evolve, the workforce will need to adapt by developing new skills. "The future of work will be about collaboration with AI," he's said, highlighting the potential for humans and AI to work together, rather than compete.

In the long run, AI will likely transform the labor market in ways we can't yet fully predict. It's possible that many jobs will become hybrid roles, where humans collaborate with AI tools to maximize productivity. As we look toward the future, it's clear that AI has the potential to not only take jobs but also create new opportunities that were once unimaginable.

NAVIGATING A CHANGING LANDSCAPE

Adapting to this new reality requires proactive steps. Reskilling and upskilling are essential for staying relevant. Learning to work with AI, whether by taking online courses in machine learning or exploring its practical applications in your industry, is as critical today as learning basic computer skills was in the 1990s.

Equally important is focusing on roles where human qualities shine. Empathy, creativity, and interpersonal skills remain difficult for AI to replicate. Careers in education, counseling, and strategic leadership—fields that require understanding and innovation—are likely to thrive in this new landscape.

AI'S ROLE ACROSS INDUSTRIES

The impact of AI isn't limited to any one sector—it's touching every corner of the economy. In healthcare, AI tools like IBM's Watson are helping doctors analyze medical records and research treatments faster than ever before. AI-powered imaging software can detect diseases like cancer and diabetic retinopathy earlier and with greater accuracy, enabling life-saving interventions.

In finance, AI is revolutionizing how we manage money. Algorithms analyze market trends, power robo-advisors for investment strategies, and flag suspicious transactions to combat fraud. Meanwhile, agriculture is seeing a tech-driven makeover. Smart drones equipped with AI sensors monitor crops, optimize irrigation schedules, and reduce pesticide use, boosting yields sustainably.

Education is also embracing AI, with adaptive learning platforms tailoring lessons to individual students' needs. Tools like these ensure that no one is left behind, providing extra support for struggling learners while challenging advanced students.

These examples illustrate that AI is not just replacing jobs—it's enhancing them, enabling professionals to work more efficiently and focus on what truly matters.

THE GLOBAL REACH OF AI'S IMPACT ON WORK

While many examples of AI advancements seem to come from the United States, the influence of AI is global. In India, for instance, e-commerce giant Flipkart uses AI to predict consumer behavior and optimize delivery logistics, a critical application in a country with over a billion people.

In the UK, AI company DeepMind is revolutionizing healthcare by developing systems that analyze medical scans for early signs of disease, significantly improving diagnosis timelines. In South Korea, Samsung employs AI to develop smart home devices that adapt to user behavior, making daily life more intuitive. And in China, Alibaba's AI innovations are not only streamlining supply chains but also enabling personalized shopping experiences for millions of users.

These global contributions highlight that AI's impact isn't confined to Silicon Valley. From Europe to Asia, countries are shaping the future of work through local ingenuity and innovation.

A NEW ERA OF WORK

The workplace is evolving rapidly, and AI is a central force behind this transformation. While some roles may disappear, others are being created, and countless more are being enhanced by AI tools. The key to thriving in this new era lies in adaptability—learning to work alongside AI rather than against it.

The next part of this book will explore how AI is enriching our personal lives, making everyday tasks more exciting, efficient, and fun. But for now, remember this: AI doesn't diminish human potential—it amplifies it.

CHAPTER

09

UNLEASHING CREATIVITY
WITH AI

AI isn't just for work—it can also fuel your creative passions, whether you're an artist, writer, musician, or simply someone who enjoys having fun with technology. From generating music to writing stories, AI tools are transforming how we approach creative expression. But can AI truly be creative, or is it just mimicking what humans have already created?

One of the most exciting ways AI is used in the creative realm is through art. While it's true that AI has been helping create more "traditional" forms of art, like visual paintings or sculptures, it's also breaking new ground with digital art and design. Tools like DeepArt and Artbreeder allow users to create stunning works of art by feeding algorithms with images, styles, and preferences. These tools use machine learning algorithms to generate new visuals based on user inputs—essentially allowing anyone, from a novice to an experienced artist, to produce pieces that would have once taken years to master.

Even more impressive is the rise of AI-powered music composition. With tools like Jukedeck, Amper Music, and OpenAI's MuseNet, creating music has become easier and more accessible. You can now generate original compositions in seconds. These AI tools analyze thousands of existing tracks across genres and then apply that knowledge to create something new. If you've ever dreamed of composing your own symphony or soundtrack but didn't know where to start, AI has opened up a whole new world of possibility. The music AI systems can produce ranges from simple melodies to complex, full-band arrangements, and it's even being used in film scores and advertising jingles.

AI's role in creative writing is also gaining momentum. While it might sound like science fiction, AI-generated text is becoming more sophisticated by the day. With the help of language models like OpenAI's GPT series (including ChatGPT), AI can write anything from articles and blog posts to entire novels. These AI systems analyze large datasets of existing text to mimic writing styles, themes, and tones, making them increasingly adept at creating human-like text. Writers are using AI to draft articles, brainstorm ideas, or even generate the basic structure of a story. In fact, some authors are experimenting with AI to co-write entire books, blending their own creativity with the AI's ability to quickly generate ideas and plot twists.

Take AI-driven poetry, for instance. Tools like AI Dungeon (an interactive storytelling game powered by GPT-3) allow users to create dynamic, interactive narratives that can adapt based on your input. Whether you're a seasoned writer or someone just playing around with the idea of telling a story, AI can offer a helpful collaborative partner—one that never runs out of ideas!

In the world of film and animation, AI is starting to play a major role in generating visuals, editing, and even producing entire short films. AI tools like Runway ML allow filmmakers and animators to create realistic special effects or enhance visuals with minimal manual effort. For example, filmmakers can use AI-powered software to alter lighting, add elements like fire or rain, or even manipulate the movement of characters within a scene. And because AI can analyze large quantities of data, it can also predict trends and audience preferences, helping creators tailor their projects to a wider demographic.

One of the most intriguing areas of AI-generated creativity is in the realm of memes. Memes have become an integral part of online culture, and AI has found its place here as well. With tools like Imgflip and Meme Generator, users can upload images and let AI generate a caption, adapting humor, wordplay, and internet culture into a fun, shareable format. It's a quick and fun way for anyone to get creative, but more importantly, it's proof that AI can understand context and style, making it more than just a tool for repetitive tasks.

While AI's creative output may sometimes seem a bit "off" or not quite as nuanced as something a human might produce, it's important to remember that AI is not replacing the creative process—it's enhancing it. AI isn't some magical artist capable of coming up with perfect art, music, or stories on its own; instead, it's an incredible tool that complements human creativity, helping to overcome creative blocks or open new pathways for exploration.

As AI becomes more advanced, there will be even more opportunities for creative people to collaborate with these tools. Whether you're generating digital art, composing music, or writing a novel, AI can take your creative projects to new heights. The best part? You don't have to be a tech expert to use these tools—many AI-powered platforms are designed to be user-friendly, accessible to anyone with an interest in creative expression. So, whether you're an aspiring musician looking for inspiration or a designer in need of a new concept, AI can provide the boost you need to make your artistic ideas come to life.

CHALLENGE TIME: GET CREATIVE WITH AI!

We've seen how AI is helping people unlock new creative potential in art, music, writing, and even memes. But now it's your turn! Don't just take my word for it—try out some of these challenges yourself and see just how fun and powerful AI can be when it comes to creativity.

Challenge 1: Make Your Own Meme

Find a funny image online (maybe something from your own camera roll!) and head to a meme generator like Imgflip or Meme Generator. Upload your image, let AI analyze it, and see what hilarious caption it suggests. Don't like the result? Fine-tune it! Edit, play around, and make your own perfect meme. Go ahead, create a meme your friends will be jealous of.

Challenge 2: Co-write a Story with AI

Ever wanted to write a short story but couldn't quite find the right words? Let AI help! Head over to a platform like AI Dungeon or even use ChatGPT to generate the beginning of a story. Try typing something like, "Start a thrilling mystery story about a detective in London." See what the AI comes up with, and then add your own twist! You could even take it a step further by asking AI to write in different genres—maybe a romance or a sci-fi tale.

Challenge 3: Compose Your Own Song

Got a favorite genre? How about a personal theme tune? Use AI tools like Jukedeck or Amper Music to create an original song. You can input your preferred style (maybe you want a rock ballad or a jazzy tune), and let AI compose something for you in minutes. Share it with friends and tell them you just became a music producer. Bonus points if you turn it into a full-blown music video using AI-generated visuals (see the section on films)!

Challenge 4: Create Digital Art

Feeling artsy? You don't need to be a professional painter to make stunning visuals. Head to platforms like DeepArt or Artbreeder, and upload a photo. Watch as the AI transforms your image into a work of art, whether it's in the style of Van Gogh or a futuristic digital painting. Play around with different effects and see what kinds of creations you can make. If you're feeling adventurous, try mixing a few styles and see what kind of unique artwork emerges!

Challenge 5: AI vs. Your Writing Style

Want to see how well AI can match your writing? Try typing a few sentences in your usual writing style, then ask an AI tool (like ChatGPT) to write in the same style. Do you notice any differences? Is the AI's tone a perfect match or does it sound like a robot trying to act like you? It's an interesting way to explore how AI analyzes and mimics writing styles. Bonus points if you try writing a paragraph with ChatGPT and then edit it to sound more like your own!

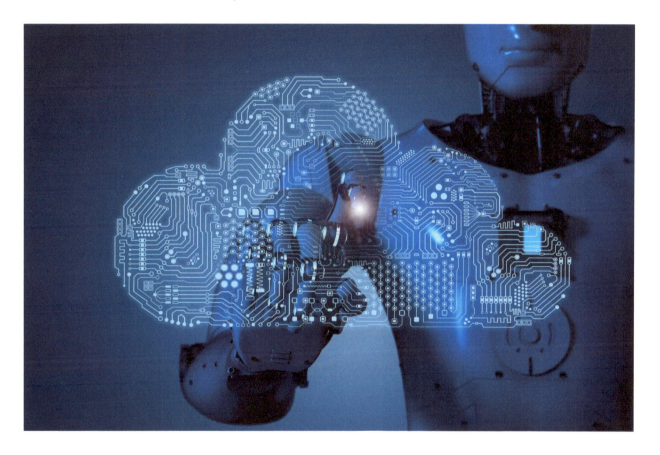

10

ETHICAL CONCERNS AND CHALLENGES

While AI offers enormous benefits, it also brings with it significant ethical concerns and potential dangers. As AI becomes more integrated into our lives, we must consider how to balance innovation with responsibility. In this section, we'll explore some of the darker sides of AI, including privacy risks, misinformation, the potential for over-reliance on machines, and concerns about cheating in education.

PRIVACY RISKS AND SURVEILLANCE

One of the most pressing concerns surrounding AI is its ability to collect and analyze vast amounts of personal data. Whether through social media, online purchases, or even our day-to-day interactions with digital assistants like Siri or Alexa, AI is constantly gathering information about us. While this data collection can be used to personalize services and improve our experience, it also opens the door to serious privacy issues.

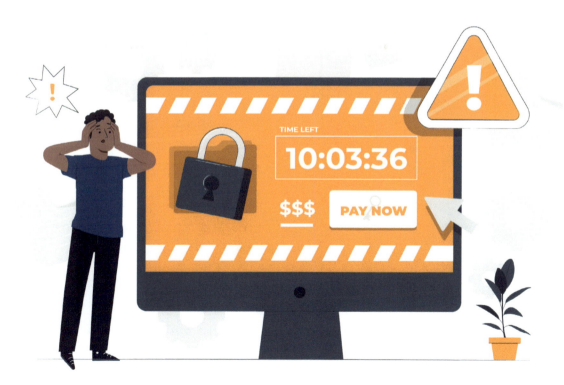

For example, AI can track our habits, preferences, and even predict our future actions. The problem arises when this data is mishandled or misused. AI-driven algorithms can make sensitive inferences about individuals based on seemingly innocuous data, like predicting health issues, financial status, or political beliefs. In the wrong hands, this information can be exploited for targeted advertising, surveillance, or even more sinister purposes.

The risk of mass surveillance is another growing concern. Governments and corporations have the potential to use AI to monitor individuals on a large scale. AI technologies such as facial recognition can be used to track people in public spaces, identify individuals from videos, and even predict behavior. While these technologies can be used for safety and security, they can also be used to infringe on personal freedoms. The idea of being constantly watched, without even realizing it, raises serious questions about our right to privacy and autonomy.

MISINFORMATION AND MANIPULATION

AI has the power to generate and spread information faster than humans ever could, but this speed comes with risks. Deepfake technology is one example of how AI can be used to create incredibly realistic but fake content—like videos or audio recordings—making it difficult for people to tell what's true and what's not. Deepfakes can be used to manipulate public opinion, damage reputations, or even sway political elections. In 2020, deepfake videos were used in political campaigns to spread misleading or false information, and the ability to create these videos continues to improve rapidly.

Beyond deepfakes, AI is also being used to spread misinformation through social media. AI algorithms, designed to optimize engagement, often amplify sensational or divisive content, making it more likely that people will be exposed to misleading or harmful information. This has been particularly concerning in the context of health misinformation, where AI-driven platforms have been used to promote dangerous conspiracy theories or unverified medical advice.

Another issue is that AI can be used to create persuasive fake news, designed to sway people's opinions on everything from political views to consumer products. These algorithms can be used to write articles or posts that seem legitimate but are ultimately designed to manipulate readers. With AI's ability to analyze and predict human emotions, it can target individuals with customized messages designed to elicit a specific response, further fueling the spread of false or harmful content.

OVER-RELIANCE ON AI

While AI can enhance our lives, there is also the risk of becoming too dependent on it. Over-relying on AI can lead to a lack of critical thinking, a loss of important human skills, and an inability to make decisions without technology. For example, AI systems are increasingly being used to make decisions in healthcare, finance, and even legal systems. While these decisions may be based on vast amounts of data and advanced algorithms, they can still be prone to errors or biases—particularly if the data being used is flawed or incomplete.

There's also the risk of AI creating a "black box" effect, where decisions made by AI systems are difficult for humans to understand or explain. For example, if an AI model in healthcare recommends a treatment plan, the reasoning behind that decision might not be easily explained to the doctor or patient. This lack of transparency can be dangerous, particularly when lives are at stake.

Additionally, as AI takes on more roles in society, there's a risk that it will replace human jobs and contribute to increased unemployment or social inequality. While AI will create new opportunities, it will also make certain job roles obsolete. As we've seen with automation in industries like manufacturing, AI has the potential to replace repetitive, manual labor. The challenge is ensuring that those displaced by AI are given the opportunity to retrain and transition to new jobs.

BIASES IN AI

Another ethical concern is the potential for biases in AI algorithms. AI systems are only as good as the data they are trained on, and if that data reflects biases—whether racial, gender-based, or socio-economic—the AI will likely reproduce those biases in its decisions. For example, studies have shown that facial recognition systems often have higher error rates for people of color, leading to concerns about racial profiling and unjust treatment. Similarly, AI-powered hiring tools have been found to favor male candidates over female ones, simply because the data they are trained on reflects historical gender imbalances.

These biases can be difficult to detect and even harder to fix, especially when the algorithms behind AI systems are proprietary or not transparent. As AI continues to play a larger role in hiring, policing, and other important areas of life, it's essential to ensure that these systems are fair and unbiased. There's a growing push for more oversight and regulation in the AI industry to prevent discrimination and ensure that AI systems are accountable for their actions.

THE CHALLENGE OF CHEATING IN EDUCATION

As AI tools become more accessible, they're increasingly being used by students for academic purposes. While AI can be a great tool for learning and research, it's also opening the door to new forms of cheating and academic dishonesty. AI-driven platforms like ChatGPT can help students complete assignments, write essays, or even generate code, raising the question: how much is too much?

In many cases, students are using AI to do the heavy lifting of their assignments, rather than learning the material themselves. This can lead to a lack of deep understanding and critical thinking. If a student relies on AI to write an essay, they miss out on the process of researching, organizing their thoughts, and developing their own ideas. The same applies to problem-solving in subjects like math or science—if a student uses AI to simply get the answer, they may struggle when faced with similar problems in the future.

Cheating with AI also poses a challenge for educators, who must find ways to detect when work has been done by a machine rather than the student. Many schools and universities are already struggling to keep up with this new form of academic dishonesty. Plagiarism detection software doesn't always catch AI-generated content, as the material is original, but may still lack the student's true input. Some educators are even concerned that students might start using AI to generate fake references or "research," making it even harder to assess the quality of their work.

But how can this be addressed? One solution is to focus more on in-class assessments and oral presentations. Teachers can engage students in real-time discussions, testing their knowledge and understanding. Instead of relying solely on written essays or reports, assignments could include interactive components where students must explain their reasoning or engage in debates on their topics.

AI can also be used in a positive way to combat cheating. There are already AI-powered tools being developed to detect AI-generated content, which could be used by educational institutions to identify students who are relying too heavily on AI. More importantly, AI could be used to enhance learning and make education more personalized. Imagine an AI tutor that adapts to a student's learning style, offering help and encouragement without doing the work for them.

ADDRESSING THE ETHICAL CHALLENGES

While these ethical concerns may seem daunting, there are steps we can take to mitigate the risks of AI. Regulation is one important tool. Governments around the world are beginning to draft laws that address issues like data privacy, transparency, and accountability for AI systems. The European Union, for example, has proposed the **Artificial Intelligence Act**, which seeks to establish clear guidelines for the use of AI and ensure that it is used in a way that protects human rights. This regulation includes provisions to classify AI systems based on their risk levels (e.g., minimal, high, or unacceptable risk) and mandate transparency and human oversight for higher-risk AI applications. It also aims to curb the use of facial recognition in public spaces, especially without consent, and establish a framework for the ethical use of AI in sectors like healthcare, transport, and employment.

In the United States, the **AI Bill of Rights** is a set of guidelines put forth by the Biden administration, emphasizing the need for fairness, accountability, and transparency in AI applications. One of the main goals is to ensure that AI doesn't exacerbate existing biases or discrimination, particularly in areas like hiring and law enforcement. The bill also advocates for consumer protection, aiming to give people control over their personal data and how it is used by AI-driven platforms.

In addition to regulatory efforts, governments are beginning to explore the use of AI to improve their own public services in ethical ways. For example, Canada has established a **Digital Charter**, which focuses on maintaining privacy while allowing businesses to innovate. The UK's **Centre for Data Ethics and Innovation** is another initiative designed to help the government navigate the ethical challenges posed by AI, advising on everything from facial recognition to AI-driven recruitment tools.

Beyond government regulations, AI developers and researchers are also working on creating more transparent and explainable AI systems. This will allow people to understand how decisions are made by AI, reducing the risk of mistakes or biases. As for the risks of misinformation, there are ongoing efforts to develop technologies that can detect and combat deepfakes and other forms of AI-generated fake content. Companies like **Microsoft** and **Adobe** are investing in AI tools that can trace the origins of images and videos, helping to authenticate content and fight misinformation.

CONCLUSION

While AI holds immense promise, it's clear that we need to approach it with caution. From the potential for privacy violations to the ethical dilemmas around misinformation and bias, there's no shortage of challenges to address. However, through thoughtful regulation, technological innovation, and responsible use, we can ensure that AI's benefits far outweigh its dangers. With the right safeguards in place, AI can help us create a better, more efficient world, without compromising our privacy, security, or ethical standards.

CHAPTER

11

THE ROAD AHEAD

AI has already changed the way we live, work, and interact with the world around us. From self-driving cars to virtual assistants, AI is woven into the fabric of our daily lives in ways that we may not even realize. But this is only the beginning. As AI continues to evolve, so too will its role in shaping our future. In this final section, we'll explore what the future of AI may look like, how we can stay informed and empowered, and what we can do to ensure AI develops in a way that benefits society as a whole.

PREDICTIONS FOR AI'S ROLE IN SOCIETY

Looking ahead, AI's potential seems limitless. But with all the excitement, there are also valid concerns. Some futurists predict that AI will revolutionize industries in ways we can't yet fully imagine. There are predictions that AI will become as essential to society as the internet is today, integrating into every aspect of our lives, from healthcare to education, from entertainment to social interaction. Yet, this future also raises critical questions about governance, regulation, and the ethics of AI use.

One area where AI is expected to have a profound impact is in **healthcare**. AI-powered diagnostics are already being used to detect diseases such as cancer, diabetes, and heart conditions earlier and more accurately than ever before. In the future, we may see AI systems that not only assist with diagnosis but also provide personalized treatment plans based on a person's genetic makeup, lifestyle, and medical history. AI could even predict health issues before they happen, offering preventive measures that could drastically improve quality of life and life expectancy.

The **automated economy** is another area where AI is poised to make waves. **Self-driving cars**, trucks, and drones are already being tested in various parts of the world, and while full autonomy may still be a few years away, many believe it's only a matter of time before AI handles a significant portion of transportation. This could lead to safer roads, more efficient logistics, and a reduction in human errors that cause accidents.

The **workplace** is also evolving rapidly as AI continues to automate routine tasks. We're already seeing the rise of AI-driven tools for **customer service**, such as chatbots that can handle inquiries and resolve issues without human intervention. In the future, entire industries may be transformed as AI takes over everything from administrative roles to complex problem-solving functions.

In **education**, AI's ability to personalize learning and adapt to individual student needs could lead to more equitable and effective learning experiences for all. With AI tutoring systems, students will receive tailored instruction, while teachers can focus more on mentoring and fostering creativity. In **arts and entertainment**, AI will continue to open up new possibilities for creating music, art, stories, and even video games, offering tools for both amateur creators and seasoned professionals alike.

Yet, as AI takes on more responsibilities, questions of control and responsibility remain. Who will be accountable when things go wrong? How will we ensure AI is used responsibly and not in ways that harm society, from deepfakes that spread misinformation to surveillance systems that infringe on privacy? The future will need to answer these questions, as it balances the potential of AI with the protection of human rights.

STAYING INFORMED AND EMPOWERED

As we move forward into a future dominated by AI, one of the most important things we can do is stay informed. AI is developing rapidly, and the better we understand how it works, the better we can prepare ourselves to use it responsibly and effectively. Fortunately, there are many ways to stay up-to-date on AI developments.

Engage with the experts:

Follow AI researchers, thought leaders, and companies at the forefront of AI innovation. This will help you keep track of the latest breakthroughs and gain insights into where AI is headed. Think of people like **Demis Hassabis**, co-founder of DeepMind, or **Fei-Fei Li**, a leading expert in computer vision, whose work is shaping the future of AI.

Educate yourself:

Take the time to learn about AI beyond what's covered in this book. There are plenty of online courses, articles, podcasts, and books that can help you understand the nuances of AI and its applications. Universities around the world offer free or affordable courses on AI and machine learning, allowing anyone to dive deeper into the subject.

Be mindful of your AI use:

As AI becomes more prevalent, it's important to approach it with an awareness of its potential risks and benefits. Understand how the AI tools you use work—whether it's a chatbot like ChatGPT, a personal assistant like Siri, or an AI-driven recommendation engine on Netflix. Knowing how these systems make decisions can help you use them more effectively and responsibly.

Get involved in discussions:

AI is not just a technological issue—it's a societal one. Engage in conversations about AI ethics, privacy, and the role of AI in society. Join online forums, attend seminars, or participate in public consultations. Your voice matters in shaping how AI evolves.

WHAT CAN YOU DO TO SHAPE AI'S FUTURE?

While AI is a powerful tool, its future development will depend largely on the actions we take today. **Governments**, **companies**, and **individuals** all have a role to play in shaping the direction AI takes. As a citizen, there are steps you can take to ensure that AI benefits society as a whole:

Support ethical AI practices:

Advocate for ethical standards in AI development, including transparency, fairness, and accountability. Support companies and organizations that prioritize responsible AI design and the ethical use of data. By voting with your wallet, you can help promote AI tools that reflect the values you care about.

Push for regulation:

Support policies that ensure AI is used responsibly. As mentioned earlier, governments around the world are beginning to draft regulations for AI to address issues like privacy, bias, and accountability. Stay informed about these initiatives and engage in discussions about how AI should be regulated.

Prepare for the future workforce:

As AI transforms the workplace, it's essential to ensure that workers are prepared for the changes ahead. Support education initiatives that help people develop the skills needed to thrive in an AI-driven world. This includes fostering interest in STEM (science, technology, engineering, and mathematics) subjects, as well as encouraging lifelong learning and adaptability.

Engage with AI in a creative way:

AI isn't just about automation—it's also about unlocking human creativity. As AI tools become more accessible, take the opportunity to explore your creative potential. Whether it's making music, creating art, or writing stories, AI can be an amazing collaborator in the creative process. By doing so, you'll better understand its capabilities and limitations, which will empower you to use it more effectively.

EMBRACING AI'S POTENTIAL

AI is already having a profound impact on our lives, and its role in the future is set to grow even more. As AI evolves, it will reshape the way we work, live, and interact with the world around us. The key to making sure AI benefits society lies in how we guide its development and use. By staying informed, advocating for responsible AI practices, and preparing ourselves for the changes ahead, we can ensure that AI becomes a powerful tool for good. The road ahead may be filled with challenges, but it's also full of exciting possibilities. Let's embrace the potential of AI, while keeping a watchful eye on its ethical implications, so that it can help us build a more equitable and prosperous future for all.

AND ONE FINAL POINT TO MAKE. GUESS WHAT? THIS BOOK WAS WRITTEN BY AI.

www.ingramcontent.com/pod-product-compliance
Lightning Source LLC
Chambersburg PA
CBHW041428050326
40689CB00003B/696